Is It Always Right To Be Right?

Warren H. Schmidt

Wadsworth Publishing Company, Inc., Belmont, California

©1970 by Wadsworth Publishing Company, Inc.
©1971 by Wadsworth Publishing Company, Inc., Belmont, California 94002.

L.C. Cat. Card No.: 72-164997

ISBN 0-534-00053-3

Printed in the United States of America

1 2 3 4 5 6 7 8 9 10 — 75 74 73 72 71

There once was a land where men were always right.

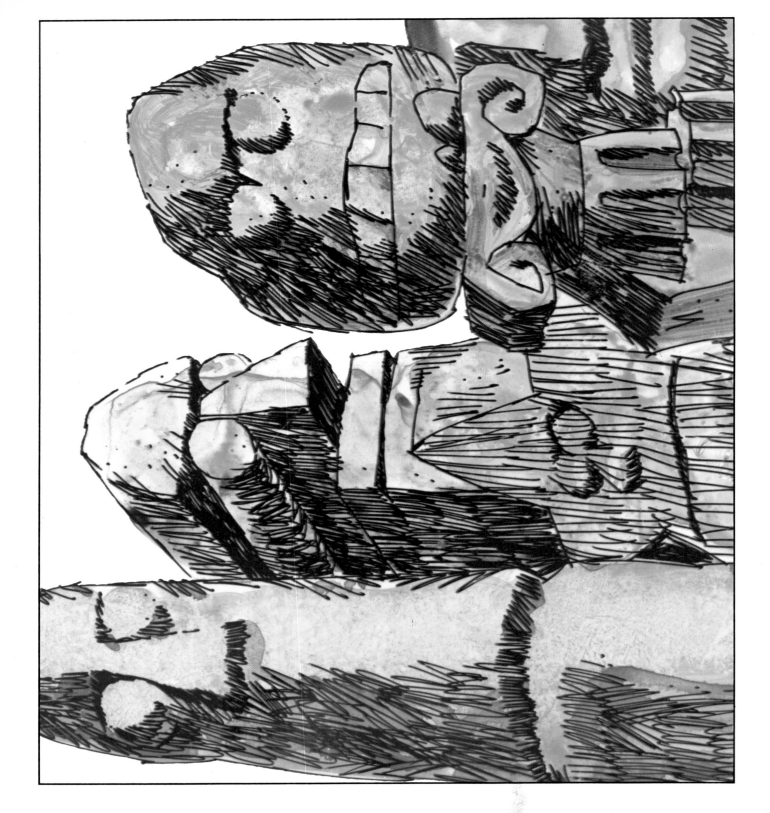

They knew it, and they were proud of it.
It was a land where a man was proud to say,

"I am right, and you are wrong."

For those were words of conviction,
strength,
and courage.

No one was ever heard to say,
"I may be wrong"
or
"You may be right."

For those were words of
weakness,
uncertainty,
and cowardice.

When differences arose between the people
of this land,

they looked not for truth, but for confirmation
of what they already believed.

When differences arose between the old and
the young, the old would say . . .

We live better than anyone in the world.

"We have worked hard to build this great and prosperous land.

We have built marvelous machines that take us wherever we want to go,

that do our work for us,

that even think.

We have gone farther,
   faster,
     deeper,
      and higher
       than anyone in history.

We expect those who inherit this good land to build on the heritage we have given them."

These older people were right, and they knew it and were proud of it.

But the younger people of that land would respond . . .

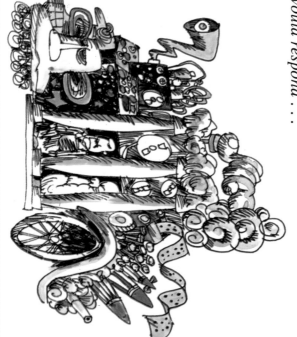

"We see around us a land that has been befouled and exploited.

People starve where food is plentiful.

Laws and practices prevent some from having an equal chance to develop and to influence.

Noble and moral words are matched by selfish and sordid deeds.

Leaders urge us to fight wars to preserve peace,

and the fighting does not end.

The whole scene is phony and polluted and inhuman and out of control.

We want no part of this money-made Establishment."

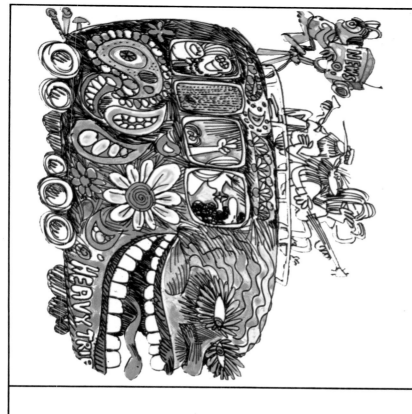

These younger people were right, and they knew it, and they were proud of it.

And a gap appeared between the generations.

When differences arose between men of different colors, those of one color would say,

"We are working steadily to build a land of justice and equality for all our citizens.

We have made considerable progress, but social progress does not come swiftly.

Those whom we seek to help and lift can only hurt their own cause when they push and intrude and pressure us.

Let them show some patience, and let them use more fully the opportunities we have already provided.

Then we will feel like doing even more for them."

These people of the majority were right, and they knew it, and they were proud of it.

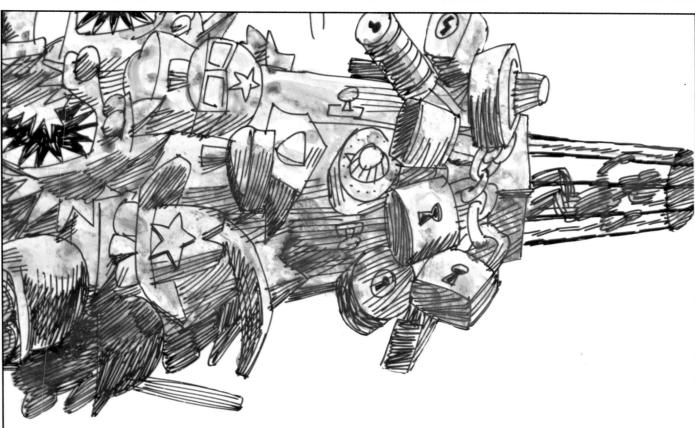

But those of another color would reply,

"We have been pushed around too long, and we are angry.

We have been confined to a ghetto.

Our children's education has been stunted in second-rate schools.

We have seen jobs go to the less qualified while our people are rejected or shunted into menial tasks.

We see a thousand subtle signs that brand us and our children as second-class citizens in this land.

We will tolerate lofty promises and meager deeds no longer."

These people from the minority were right, and they knew it and were proud of it.

It happened to those who gave priority to a strong defense and those who gave priority to better cities.

And the gap between the races grew.

And so it went in this land . . . . .

Group after group defined the right and took their stand and upheld their position against those who opposed them.

It happened between those who taught in schools and those who provided the funds.

It happened to those who pleaded for peace at any price and those who argued for national honor at any cost.

Everyone was right, and they knew it, and they were proud of it.

And the gap grew wider. . .

until the day came when all activity stopped.

Each group stood in its solitary rightness, glaring with proud eyes at those too blind to see their *truth.*

They were determined to maintain their position at all costs — for this is the responsibility of being right.

No one travelled across the giant gap.

No one talked to those on the other side.

No one listened.

The quality of life declined and became grim.

. . . . .

Then, one day, a strange new sound was heard in the land.

Someone said, "I may be wrong."

At first the people were shocked that anyone could be so weak and so confused.

Then another voice said,

"You may be right."

The people burst into laughter to hear anyone so indecisive and soft.

They even began to see signs of humanity and noble purpose in those whom they once knew only as adversaries.

But the voice persisted and some began to listen. They began to listen to opposing and even "wrong" views. As they listened,

they discovered common beliefs they had not known before.

Here and there men expressed their common desires in deeds — and bright examples of joint action were seen in the land.

With each new effort, men's faith in one
another grew,

and their faith in the future

and their ability to shape their own destiny.

They stated these beliefs in a Declaration
of Interdependence . . .

All men are created equal — but each develops
in a unique way.

All men are endowed with certain inalienable
rights — but each must assume certain inevitable
responsibilities.

For the happiness of all depends on the commitment
of each to support equality and difference, rights and
responsibilities.

In this land men had learned how two rights could
make a costly wrong. That it may take less courage to
point the finger of blame than to extend the
hand of partnership and less wisdom to defend a
narrow right than to seek a broader understanding.

Most important of all, the people of this land
had learned that the quest for truth is never over . . .
that the challenge is always the same . . .

To stop fighting long enough to listen

To learn from those who differ

To try new approaches

To seek and test new relationships

And to keep at a task that never ends . . . .   *Not the end...*